SQUADRONS!

No. 15

The Gloster Meteor F. I & F. III

Phil H. LISTEMANN

ISBN: 978-2918590-94-1

Copyright

© 2016 Philedition - Phil Listemann

updated December 2018, revised December 2021

Colour profiles: Bill Dady /clavework-graphics

All right reserved. No part of this book may be reproduced, stored in a retrieval system or transmitted in any form by any means, electronic, mechanical, photocopying, recording or otherwise, without prior permission of the author.

Contributors & Acknowledgments:
Andrew Thomas, Chris Thomas, Donald Nijboer

GLOSSARY OF TERMS

PERSONEL :

(AUS)/RAF: Australian serving in the RAF
(BEL)/RAF: Belgian serving in the RAF
(CAN)/RAF: Canadian serving in the RAF
(CZ)/RAF: Czechoslovak serving in the RAF
(NFL)/RAF: Newfoundlander serving in the RAF
(NL)/RAF: Dutch serving in the RAF
(NZ)/RAF: New Zealander serving in the RAF
(POL)/RAF: Pole serving in the RAF
(RHO)/RAF: Rhodesian serving in the RAF
(SA)/RAF: South African serving in the RAF
(US)/RAF - RCAF : American serving in the RAF or RCAF

RANKS

G/C : Group Captain
W/C : Wing Commander
S/L : Squadron Leader
F/L : Flight Lieutenant
F/O : Flying Officer
P/O : Pilot Officer
W/O : Warrant Officer
F/Sgt : Flight Sergeant
Sgt : Sergeant
Cpl : Corporal
LAC : Leading Aircraftman

OTHER

ATA: Air Transport Auxiliary
CO : Commander
DFC : Distinguished Flying Cross
DFM : Distinguished Flying Medal
DSO : Distinguished Service Order
Eva. : Evaded
ORB : Operational Record Book
OTU : Operational Training Unit
PoW : Prisoner of War
PAF: Polish Air Force
RAF : Royal Air Force
RAAF : Royal Australian Air Force
RCAF : Royal Canadian Air Force
RNZAF : Royal New Zealand Air Force
SAAF : South African Air Force
s/d: Shot down
Sqn : Squadron
† : Killed

CODENAMES - OFFENSIVE OPERATIONS - FIGHTER COMMAND

CIRCUS:
Bombers heavily escorted by fighters, the purpose being to bring enemy fighters into combat.

RAMROD:
Bombers escorted by fighters, the primary aim being to destroy a target.

RANGER:
Large formation freelance intrusion over enemy territory with aim of wearing down enemy figthers.

RHUBARD:
Freelance fighter sortie against targets of opportunity.

RODEO:
A fighter sweep without bombers.

SWEEP:
An offensive flight by fighters designed to draw up and clear the enemy from the sky.

THE GLOSTER METEOR

The Gloster Meteor was the first British jet fighter and the Allies' only operational jet aircraft during the Second World War. The development of the turbojet-powered Meteor was a collaboration between the Gloster Aircraft Company and Frank Whittle's firm, Power Jets Ltd. Frank Whittle formed Power Jets in March 1936, to develop his ideas of jet propulsion, and served as the company's chief engineer. At the end of the thirties, Britain and Germany were at the forefront of jet-powered aircraft development. In late 1939, the Air Ministry contracted Gloster to manufacture a prototype aircraft powered by one of Whittle's new engines. In August 1940, Gloster presented its initial proposals for a twin-engine jet fighter with a nose-wheel (tricycle) undercarriage. On 6 February 1941, Gloster received an order for twelve prototypes, **DG202-213** (later reduced to eight), under Specification F9/40. A letter of intent for the production of 300 of the new fighter was issued. The naming of the aircraft did not prove straightforward, with 'Avenger', 'Scourge', 'Terrifer', 'Thunderbolt' and 'Tempest' being considered, before 'Meteor' was settled upon. During the aircraft's secretive development, employees and officials made use of the codename 'Rampage' in reference to their work. Test locations and other key project information were similarly obscured.

For the Meteor, the main issue was to find the right engines and the development of these took more time than initially planned and proved more complicated than originally thought. The first Meteor to fly was DG206 on 5 March 1943 when it took to the sky for a mere three minutes and thirty seconds! Knowing that the first taxi runs were carried out the previous summer clearly shows the difficulties encountered leading to the first flight. A summary of the career of the eight prototypes will help to have a better understanding of the matter:

DG202: First flew on 24.07.43 with W.2B/23 engines.
DG203: First flew on 09.11.43 with W.2/500 engines.
DG204: First flew on 13.11.43 with Metropolitan-Vickers F.2 engines. During a subsequent flight, the compressor failed and the pilot, Squadron Leader William D.B.S. Davie, abandoned the aircraft over Farnborough on 4 January 1944. He did not survive.
DG205: First flew on 12.06.43 with W.2B/23 engines. Used by Gloster for handling trials, it would be lost in a crash the following 27 April, killing Gloster pilot J.A. Crosby-Warren.
DG206: First flew on 05.03.43 with Halford H.1 engines.
DG207: First flew on 24.07.45 as the Meteor F.2 prototype.
DG208: First flew on 20.01.44 with W.2B/23 engines.
DG209: First flew on 18.04.44 with W.2B/37 engines.
DG210 was not completed and DG211 to DG213 cancelled.

F9/40 Meteor DG202/G was the first prototype powered by Rover W.2B engines. The photo was taken in July 1943 at the time it made its first flight. The fin/tailplane does not have the acorn fillet that was added later.

Above, the third prototype, DG204/G, was powered by Metro-Vick F.2 axial-flow engines in underwing nacelles and, below, F9/40 prototype DG206/G powered by Hatford H.1 turbojets. The letter 'G' after the serials indicates the aircraft had to be guarded permanently when on the ground.

Eventually it was decided that the W.2B would be the engines installed on the production version, the Meteor F.1.

During the war, the following contracts were placed:
- In August 1941, 300 aircraft (**EE210-254, EE269-318, EE331-369, EE384-429, EE444-493, EE517-554, EE568-599**), split in two marks, 200 F.1s and 100 F.2s. When the F.2 was cancelled the order reverted to 300 F.1s. Eventually, this order was delivered as twenty F.1s between February and September 1944, and 230 F.3s of which 111 were delivered before VJ-Day (2 September 1945).
- In August 1943, 100 Meteor F.2s (**RA365-398, RA413-457, RA473-493**) but this batch would be eventually delivered as F.4s after the war.
- In February 1945, 300 Meteor F.3s (**TX386-428, TX531-567, TX572-614, TX618-645, TX649-688, TX693-737, TX739-776, TX779-804**). All cancelled following the end of the war in September 1945.

The Marks:

F.1:
The designation F.1 was allocated to the first production version of the Meteor. All early production Meteors had provision to be powered by either the Whittle W.2B or W.2/500 engine. In April 1943, the production order was temporarily cut from 300 to just twenty, a situation that came from the various delays and also doubts regarding whether the program would go the distance. In the end only these twenty were to be built with serials EE210 to EE229. The first production Meteor, EE210, was flown on 12 January 1944 and, apart from the armament of four 20mm cannons in the nose and the two W.2B/23 engines of 1,700 lb thrust each, it was in all respects a duplicate of DG202. However, because the development process associated with this new form of propulsion was so extensive, numerous F.1s joined the prototypes in the test program with several going to RAE Farnborough or A&AEE at Boscombe Down. Therefore, six Meteors never reached an operational unit, EE210, EE211, EE212, EE213, EE214 and EE223, while six others were used operationally and as test aircraft (EE215, EE216, EE217, EE219, EE221 and EE227). It was armed with four 20mm Hispano cannons with a total of 780 rounds.

F.2:
This mark was intended to be the version powered by the de Havilland H.1 Goblin engine, the engine that was allocated to the DH.100 Vampire. The performance was actually very similar to the F.1 but it was for industrial considerations, not technical considerations, that the F.2 was never built and remained at the prototype stage (see above).

F.3:
This mark could be seen as the true first operational version. It was intended to be powered by the 2,000 lb thrust Rolls-Royce W.2B/37 'Derwent 1' engine first tested in DG209. However, production of these engines encountered delays and, not wanting to hinder the delivery of the Meteor to the RAF, an interim measure was found and the first fifteen F.3s received the W.2B/23c (EE230-EE244). This version also introduced a new canopy.

The Gloster Meteor became the first British jet fighter and was to have a long career in the RAF, built in many different versions, flying a variety of roles, and widely exported. However, it never had the chance to fight against manned German aircraft, particularly the Me262, to prove just how advanced it was. As a fighter, and the RAF was well aware of this, it could not hope replace the entire fighter force in the future because, like all twin-engine aircraft, it lacked the maneuverability of single engine fighters. It was a big disadvantage against the soon-to-be-in-service single engine Vampire. It was also more costly to operate. Without a doubt, though, it heralded a new era for the RAF.

Meteor EE211/G was the second production Meteor F. 1. Completed on 14 March 1944, EE211 made its first flight one month later. It was initially retained by Gloster and in July 1944 was transferred to RAE Farnborough for extensive trials. It is seen here with airflow tufts attached to the port wing and engine nacelle. EE211 would become an instructional airframe between April 1946 and April 1952.
(Donald Nijboer's collection)

In January 1945, EE227 left No. 616 Squadron to serve for various experiments. EE227 received initially a T-tail and in this form it became the only T-tail Meteor and the first British T-tailed turbojet aircraft. This modification offered virtually nothing on the way of improvements and the idea was abandoned. Afterwards in March 1945 EE227 went to Rolls-Royce to have two RB.50 Trent propeller turbines installed. As such it became the first aircraft in the world to fly with a propeller driven by a gas turbine, a type of powerplant which today is called a turboprop.

July 1944
August 1945

Victories - confirmed or probable claims: 13.0 V1-s

First operational sortie: F.1: 27.07.44 F.3: 03.03.45 **Last operational sortie:** F.1: 03.09.44 F.3: 04.05.45	**Number of sorties: 531** F.1: 286, F.3: 245 **Total aircraft written-off: 5** Aircraft lost on operations: 3 (1 F.1) Aircraft lost in accidents: 2 (both F.1s)

Squadron code letters:
YQ

COMMANDING OFFICERS

W/C Andrew McDowall	RAF No. 89299	RAF	23.07.44	03.05.45
W/C Warren E. Schrader	NZ411944	RNZAF	03.05.45	...

SQUADRON USAGE

This unit would become the first squadron to receive the new jet fighter and also the first to become operational. The squadron already had a long military history when the first two Meteor F.1s were taken on charge. Based at Manston, the squadron was, at that time, part of ADGB (soon to become Fighter Command again) and was equipped with Spitfire Mk. VIIs, a type that was at the end of its service life with the RAF (see SQUADRONS! No. 6). With the impending arrival of the Meteors, Wing Commander McDowall arrived, to become the first CO of a jet fighter squadron, and took over from Squadron Leader Leslie Watts (who remained with 616). Indeed, considering the Meteor was a twin-engine aircraft, command of the squadron required a wing commander. McDowell was a very experienced pilot, with a DFM and Bar to his name, and was seen as the best man to lead the first jet-powered unit of the RAF. While continuing operations over the Continent, the first two Meteors (EE213 and EE214) arrived at the squadron on 21 July which were easily recognised by their yellow bellies. Both were actually on A&AEE charge and were not able to carry out a single operational sortie. Of course this arrival caused great interest, as well as excitement, at the Station and soon both aircraft were put undercover in a

> A very important factor in the introduction of the Meteor to operational service was Wing Commander Hugh 'Willie' Wilson. A fighter pilot who left the RAF in 1934, he was recalled to active service at the outbreak of war. Because he had worked at Blackburn Aircraft (he had been the test pilot of the Roc), he was posted to the Aeronautical Flight of the RAE at Farnborough and later flew the various captured aircraft types that passed through that unit. He was then deeply involved in the Meteor program and was tasked to supervise the training of 616's pilots during their conversion in July 1944. He flew EE221/HJW while attached to 616. In November 1945 he set a world air speed record for a jet fighter of 606.38 miles per hour (975.87 km/h) in Meteor IV EE454 (the Mk. IV prototype) while OC of the ETPS (Empire Test Pilots' School). He left the RAF soon after to return to Blackburn Aircraft.

A Gloster Meteor F.1, of 616 Sqn, coming in to land at Manston, Kent. The individual letters known to have been allocated were: EE213/A, EE214/B, EE215/C, EE216/E, EE217/J, EE218/F, EE219/D (later N), EE220/G, EE221/C (later HJW), EE222/G, EE224/O, EE227/Y, EE229/W.

hangar and guarded by Security Police. Two days later, five Meteors arrived (EE215, EE216, EE217, EE218, EE219) and these were operational. All had passed through A&AEE or RAE hands. The F.1 was still seen as a pre-production aircraft and 616 would work closely with Gloster, and the various RAF establishments like the A&AEE or the RAE, over the next few weeks. The squadron worked with three flights, two being still operational on Spitfires, while the 'new' flight prepared for operational Meteor flying. The next few days concentrated on converting the pilots and, on the 26th, the 'Meteor Flight' was declared operational with the aim to defend Great Britain against the latest of Hitler's weapons, the V-1. By July, the RAF was approaching the height of its V-1 interceptions and it was a good time for the Meteors and its pilots to experience operational conditions. The Flight included the following pilots: W/C McDowall, S/L 'Watty' Watts, F/L Mike Cooper, F/Os 'Dixie' Dean, J.K. Rodger and 'Mac' McKenzie (a Canadian), P/O Clerc, (a Frenchman) and W/O G.M. Wilkes. History was made the next day when, at 14.30, F/O McKenzie took off to patrol a line between Ashford and Robertsbridge where the V-1 bombs were often encountered. This patrol was uneventful. Five other patrols were carried out that day by the Flight and S/L Watts was close to opening the Meteor's score against the V-1 but his cannons failed, while F/O Dean was able to close to 1,000 yards of another when he was called back by control because of the proximity of balloons.

EE227/QY-Y seen at Manston in September 1944 at a time when the V-1 threat had reached its end (or very near to it).

Gloster Meteor F.1s of 616 Sqn, based at Manston, Kent, in flight over the countryside between West Hougham and Dover, ever ready to intercept V-1s.

Extracted from a cine-film showing Meteor EE214 in the standard non-operational colour scheme for day fighters with Trainer yellow undersides. The faired-over guns ports indicated that EE214 was not armed. The codes QY-B are also visible.
Below EE217 taken shortly after its arrival at 616 Squadron.
(Donald Nijboer's collection - both)

Command of 616 Sqn was given to Wing Commander McDowall, a very experienced pilot with a DFM & Bar (a rare combination for a fighter pilot) awarded while serving with 602 Sqn during the Battle of Britain, and with a score of more than ten kills. After the war, thanks to the experience earned while with 616, he went to work for Glosters where he tested Meteors being sold to foreign air forces.

Patrols continued the next day between 08.00 and 17.45, with each of approximately of 40-45 minutes duration. No success was recorded. However, the squadron was reinforced when two more Meteors, EE220 and EE221, arrived. On the 29th, operational activity was maintained between 10.25 and 22.10, but was performed alongside test flights. It was during one such test that the Meteor fired its guns in anger for the first time. While conducting an engine test, W/C Wilson sighted one 'Diver' at 2,000 feet near Rye and estimated its speed at 360 mph on a course of 360°. He opened fire but was out of range and eventually lost the V-1 in cloud. The only other pilot who made contact with a V-1 during the day was the Frenchman Clerc, but he was unable to engage. The next day another contact was made, by F/O Dean who fired at a V-1, but the results were unobserved. A low ceiling prevented operational flights on the 31st.

In August, anti-Diver sorties became the routine with the number depending on the weather and visitors coming to see the new aircraft. At the same time, more pilots became operational on the Meteor. There were more unsuccessful contacts on the first day of August, but the first kill was at last recorded on the 4th when F/O Dean became the first pilot to make a claim while flying the Meteor. He had taken off from Manston at 15.45 to patrol once more when, at 16.16, a V-1 was sighted at 1,000 feet near Tonbridge on a course of 330° and at an estimated speed of 365 mph. Dean dived from 4,500 feet at a speed of 450 mph and attacked the flying bomb from dead astern. His cannons failed to fire so he decided to manoeuver alongside the V-1 and change its course by placing his wing under the bomb's wing and pulling upwards at the same time. He saw the V-1 hit the ground four miles from Tonbridge. The day wasn't over and, a few minutes later, it was F/O 'Jock' Rodger's turn to attack another V-1 that he shot down with his guns. From that moment, successes against the V-1s mounted with one being shot down on the 7th, again by Dean, but this time using his can-

W/C McDowall's Meteor F.1 in July-August 1944 was EE222/G coded YQ-G. It would be lost on 29 August 1944 after an anti-Diver patrol. *(Andrew Thomas)*

Meteor F.1s of 616 Sqn, with EE219/D in the foreground, lined-up at Manston in January 1945. *(Andrew Thomas)*

Below, another scene of 616 Sqn's Meteors in January 1945. These are Meteor F.1s and Welland-powered F.3s, with EE235/P (a F.3) and EE229/W (a F.1) just behind. A further F.3, EE234/YQ-O, can be identified facing the opposite direction to the other Meteors. Just behind YQ-W, and partially obscured, is EE239/Q which would later be painted white while stationed on the Continent. *(CT Collection)*

Ground crew refuelling Gloster Meteor F.3, EE236/YQ-H. It served as an instructional airframe from January 1945.

nons which didn't jam. He claimed a third V-1 on the 10th. By that time, 616 was solely a Meteor unit having received more jets and the Spitfire VIIs being disposed of. At about that time, though, the squadron recorded its first Meteor loss when F/Sgt D.A. Gregg was killed in EE226. He took off from Manston for High Halden to begin his readiness (High Halden was the other airfield where the Meteors were operating). It seems he got lost and could not find the airfield. He tried to land at Great Chart airfield, near Ashford, but crashed on making his approach. He was the RAF's first jet fatality. The next day was a busy one for the squadron, with 23 patrols or scrambles, during which two more V-1s were destroyed (one each for McKenzie (RCAF) and Mullenders, a Belgian). McDowall was unlucky that day as he was unable to make any hits despite two encounters. On the 17th, three more V-1s were added (F/O Ritch (RCAF), W/O Woodacre and F/Sgt Easy). The same day, EE224 was accidentally damaged by cannon from EE225 while parked at dispersal. The Meteor was sent to Gloster but was finally not repaired. The claims made the 17th were followed by three on the 19th (two for F/O Hobson, one shared, and one for F/Sgt Watts) and one more on the 28th shared by F/O Hobson and F/Sgt Epps. The last for the month was claimed on the next day by F/O Miller. That same day, W/C McDowall ran out of fuel after a long anti-Diver patrol and had to make a belly landing in a field near Pucks Gutter but he escaped injury. The aircraft was unrepairable. In all, about 230 sorties were carried out that month during which 13 V-1s were claimed as destroyed. What was unknown at that time, however, was that the Meteor F.1's war was over.

Anti-Diver patrols or scrambles were only carried out on first three days of September for a total of 29 sorties. The rest of the month was spent in practice and other non-operational flights. An important detachment of four aircraft was mounted early in the month

Ground crew pushing Meteor YQ-Q. Now painted white, the only remaining markings are the national insignia and the letter 'Q' painted on the nose wheel door. This Meteor would also eventually become an instructional airframe.

A Gloster Meteor F.3, of the 616 Sqn detachment, takes off from B58/Melsbroek, Belgium, shortly after joining No. 84 Group of 2 TAF in the air defence role. In the foreground a mobile Chance light stands parked by the main runway and, as can be seen, the Meteors were painted white to aid in their identification.

to the American airfield of Debden. The appearance of the Me262 in German skies had caused a lot of concerns within the USAAF so plans were organised to evaluate the combat capabilities of enemy jet fighters and determine defensive and offensive tactics for the bombers and their fighter escorts. The four pilots selected for this exercise were the CO, S/L Barry, F/L Gosling and P/O Stodhart. During the exercises, the Meteor performed well in dogfights as long as the speed was kept high. For the rest of the month, and into November and December, the Meteors were in regular demand by the RAF and USAAF alike for tactical training. In December, 616 began to receive the first F.3s, EE231 and EE232. These were still powered by the Welland engines due to the slow delivery of the more powerful Rolls-Royce Derwents. Following the first two, three more arrived on the 24th, EE234, EE235 and EE238, and two on the 28th (EE236 and EE237). More F.3s were taken on charge in January and February 1945, progressively replacing the F.1. The last of the original aircraft finally left on 10 March for newly formed 1335 CU.

In the meantime, it had been decided that the Meteor F.3 would be used on operations on the Continent with 2 TAF so the squadron was transferred to 84 Group. The advance party of fifty men left on 28 January for Melsbroek (B-58) in Belgium, the new home for the Meteor. On 4 February, the first four aircraft, led by the OC (in EE225, the other pilots being Dennis Berry in EE239, F/L Mullenders in EE240, and F/O JK Rodgers in EE241), made the first trip and, upon arrival, they were painted white to avoid any confusion with the Me262. Flights were also scheduled to be flown over Allied lines at appointed times so that Allied personnel could become accustomed with the sight of the Meteor. McDowell returned to the UK a couple of days later. The move was slow, however, due to bad weather over the Continent for most of the month. Another event put a halt to this move as the V-1 re-appeared over the British Isles obliging the squadron to maintain Meteors at home for this new threat. Contrary to the previous summer, little activity was recorded and only thirteen sorties were flown until 19 March when a handful of V-1 sightings were made, but none were shot down. The priority changed, therefore, and the move to the Continent accelerated and was eventually completed when of the remaining aircraft (in all seventeen) were in place on the 31st.

The first operational sorties flown from Belgium took place on 3 April when F/L Mike Cooper (from Kenya) and 'Dixie' Dean took off at 16.50 after red flares were fired from flying control. Since that morning, the squadron had had two aircraft permanently on standby. They were vectored over Brussels where they intercepted two friendly aircraft and returned to base at 17.20. Until the 16th, the Meteors only scrambled a couple of times and each sortie was uneventful. The RAF was reluctant to use the Meteor on offensive operations over enemy territory. Danger could also come from friendly gunners who occasionally fired at the Meteors despite the white paint. By mid-April, the end of war was so close that the RAF cleared the Meteor for use over enemy held territory. Even

Les Watts fought with 603 and 249 Sqns during the worst months of the Malta siege in 1942 and was able to make several claims. For his second tour, he was posted to 616 Sqn in June 1943, then 322 (Dutch) Sqn, as a flight commander before returning to 616 as CO. He remained with the squadron and later transitioned to the Meteor but would find his death on 29.04.45 during an evening patrol. He was one of only two F.3 wartime operational losses for the Meteor.

should a Meteor fall into German hands, the consequences would be non-existent. On the 16th, led by S/L Watts, eight Meteors took off at 11.55 for an armed reconnaissance. This was the first offensive mission ever carried out by the Meteor. The formation returned to base after 45 minutes with nothing to report. At that moment, the white paint became useless and, as the recently arrived Meteors were painted in standard camouflage, the Meteors that had received the white paint were sent back to Colerne to have it removed. Until the end of the hostilities in Europe, the Meteor would be mainly engaged in ground attack operations. A few moves took place; on the 13th to B-91/Kluis, the 20th to B-109/Quakenbrück, and B-156/Fassberg on 3 May. Quakenbrück and Fassberg were in Germany. The first success came on the 17th when F/L Cooper destroyed an enemy truck. By the end of April, 116 sorties were flown with good results on the ground and no Meteor lost during the offensive sorties. However, the end of the month would close on a dramatic event when two Meteors collided during an evening patrol. Having taken off at 19.20 for a routine patrol, neither of the two pilots, S/L Watts and F/Sgt B. Cartmel, would ever return. It came to light later on, via the radio control centre, that Spitfire pilots flying in the area heard Watts calling Cartmel to come closer as he was going into cloud. Shortly afterwards they saw a large explosion in the air. As April ended, a new commander arrived at the squadron, Wing Commander W.E. 'Smokey' Schrader DFC, a New Zealander with thirteen victories to his tally, from No. 486 (NZ) Squadron where he had been flying the Tempest.

Even as the war in Europe was in its very last days, 616 carried out no less than 92 sorties, in four days, during which dozens of vehicles were destroyed or damaged. For example, on 2 May, the pilots claimed twenty vehicles destroyed and 100 more damaged. That day, the Meteor came close to claiming its first air victory as a Storch was seen on the return leg and was attacked by F/L

Tony Jennings. For the Storch, it was easy to counter the attacks, turning towards its attacker as the Meteor reached firing range, so Jennings could not get in to a good position to open fire. The fight ended when the German pilot decided not dare the Meteor pilot any further and landed in a field. The two persons on board escaped before Jennings made a strafing pass and destroyed the Fi-156. The following day, during a surprise attack against the airfield of Schönberg, one Fieseler Storch, two Ju87s, two He111s and one Bf109 were destroyed on the ground. All but the Storch were destroyed at the airfield. The next day, the 4th, the Meteors were responsible for the destruction of more targets to bring the total for May to 43 motor vehicles, two locos and seven aircraft on the ground. The new CO was lucky as he ran out of fuel but managed a successful dead-stick landing at base. At 17.00 the message announcing the end of the hostilities in Northern Europe was received and no more sorties were therefore carried out. On 7 May, the squadron moved to Lubeck (B-158), a base it would stay at until 30 August when it was renamed No. 263 Squadron. In all, the Meteor F.1 and F.3 achieved a modest tally of just less than 500 operational sorties and more than a dozen V-1s claimed. Most importantly, the RAF had entered in the jet age.

The last wartime CO of 616 was 'Smokey' Schrader. He was a New Zealander who started his wartime career in the UK with 165 Sqn in 1942 before sailing to Malta where he joined 1435 Sqn. In March 1945, he began his last tour of operations flying Tempests with 486 (NZ) Sqn and, in a couple of weeks, would become one of the most successful Tempest pilots in claiming ten enemy destroyed (one being shared). He ended the war with a DFC & Bar.
(via Paul Sortehaug)

Claims - 616 Squadron (Confirmed and Probable)

Date	Pilot	SN	Origin	Type	Serial	Code	Nb	Cat.
04.08.44	F/O Thomas D. Dean	RAF No. 159492	RAF	V-1	EE216	YQ-E	1.0	C
	F/O John K. Rodger	RAF No. 139638	RAF	V-1			1.0	C
07.08.44	F/O Thomas D. Dean	RAF No. 159492	RAF	V-1			1.0	C
10.08.44	F/O Thomas D. Dean	RAF No. 159492	RAF	V-1			1.0	C
16.08.44	F/O William H. McKenzie	Can./ J.16763	RCAF	V-1	EE225		0.5	C
	F/O Marcel P.M.A. Mullenders	RAF No. 126129	(Bel)/RAF	V-1			1.0	C
17.08.44	F/O Jack R. Ritch	Can./ J.2223	RCAF	V-1	EE217	YQ-J	1.0	C
	W/O Thomas S. Woodacre	RAF No. 1379827	RAF	V-1	EE218	YQ-F	1.0	C
	F/Sgt Raymond C.H. Easy	RAF No. 571293	RAF	V-1			1.0	C
19.08.44	F/O Gordon N. Hobson	RAF No. 136445	RAF	V-1	EE217	YQ-J	1.5	C
	F/Sgt Philip G. Watts	RAF No. 1177637	RAF	V-1			1.0	C
28.08.44	F/O Gordon N. Hobson	RAF No. 136445	RAF	V-1	EE217	YQ-J	0.5	C
	F/Sgt Edwin H.T. Epps	RAF No. 575364	RAF	V-1			0.5	C
29.08.44	F/O Hugh Miller	RAF No. 158323	RAF	V-1			1.0	C

Total: 13.0

Summary of the aircraft lost on Operations - 616 Squadron

Date	Pilot	S/N	Origin	Serial	Code	Fate
29.08.44	W/C Andrew McDowall	RAF No. 89299	RAF	EE222	YQ-G	-
29.04.45	S/L Leslie W. Watts	RAF No. 117728	RAF	EE252	YQ-G	†
	F/Sgt Brian Cartmel	RAF No. 1512014	RAF	EE273	YQ-K	†

Total: 3

F. 1: EE222, F.3: EE252 & EE273

Summary of the aircraft lost by accident - 616 Squadron

Date	Pilot	S/N	Origin	Serial	Code	Fate
15.08.44	F/Sgt Donald A. Gregg	RAF No. 1235043	RAF	EE226		†
17.08.44	-	-	RAF	EE224	YQ-O	-

Total: 2

Both EE224 & EE226: F.1

No. 616 Sqn's two-letter code 'YQ' is carefully applied to an Meteor F.1. *(Donald Nijboer's collection)*

Three photos of Meteor F.3s while stationed in Germany during the summer of 1945. Top, EE275/YQ-Q arrived in March 1945 to replace an F.3 powered by the Whittle engines. It was later re-coded HE-Q when 616 became 263 at the end of August 1945. EE275 would have a long career with the RAF and was withdrawn from use in April 1954 and scrapped the following August.

Left, EE278/YQ-G was also delivered in March 1945 and would serve with various squadrons - 263 (ex-616), 257, 222 and 1 - and ended as an advanced trainer at 206 AFS. Withdrawn from use in June 1953, it became an instructional airframe in December 1954.

Below, EE249/YQ-N arrived in February 1945 and was still with the squadron when it was re-numbered 263 in August 1945. A victim of an accident in January 1946, it was stored for two years after repairs were undertaken before being returned to service with second line units. Stored for a final time in May 1952, it was sold for scrap in October 1955.
(Chris Thomas)

With the other units

With the operational trials proving conclusive and production going ahead, the need to form a unit to convert pilots onto the Meteor became clear at the beginning of 1945. Number 616 Squadron converted all of its pilots but, for the other units, something else had to be found. The solution came with the formation of No. 1335 (Meteor) Conversion Unit on 8 March 1945 at Colerne. The initial establishment was eight Meteor F.1s, now withdrawn from the front line, and six Meteor F.3s. The latter were the ones equipped with the same engines as the F.1s. Also, to ease the conversion on to twin-engine procedures, the CU was to receive four Oxfords and four Martinets. The Meteors assigned to the new units were EE216, EE217, EE218, EE220, EE225, EE228 and EE229 (all on 10.03.45). The CU never received its eighth F.1 and, furthermore, would soon lose EE225 before the end of the month as it was converted to an instructional airframe due to the need to train the fitters at the same time! The consignment of F.3s was received the same day with EE231, EE232 (soon transferred to the CFE), EE233, EE234, EE236, EE237, EE242 and EE244 making the fourteen Meteors (EE238 replaced EE232 on 29.03.45). On 12 April, the number of Meteors was increased to eighteen with the arrival of EE235, EE239, EE240 and EE241. However, that number was on paper only as the previous day EE234 had been in an accident when W/O R. Marr (RAAF) overshot on a single engine landing at Colerne. The pilot had to raise the undercarriage to stop the machine. EE234 was sent to Glosters one week later and never flew again as it was converted into an instructional airframe. No major changes would occur until the end of war but various accidents reduced the number of Meteors at the CU. On 15 April, it was the turn of EE217 to be the victim of an accident. It was also sent for repairs at Glosters, but returned to the RAF in October 1945. The left engine of EE228 caught fire while taxiing on 2 August. The aircraft was sent to Glosters, but by then the F.1 was totally obsolete and the decision was made not to repair the airframe. EE228 would become another instructional airframe. More dramatic was the loss of EE238 on 18 May when the pilot, W/C Alan S. Dredge, lost control in a barrel roll during a demonstration at Farnborough and flew into the ground. He was killed instantly. Dredge was a former Typhoon pilot who had been awarded the DFC, while serving with No. 183 Squadron, and the DSO while commanding No. 3 Squadron. In June and July, the CU was reinforced as EE239, EE240 and 241 left the unit and were replaced by EE315, EE316, EE318, EE331, EE347, EE349, EE351 to EE357.

Another unit used the Meteor in numbers before the end of war. The CFE (Central Fighter Establishment) at Tangmere formed in

Above: Gloster Meteor F.3 EE317 taken in flight wearing the codes of 1335 CU (XL-Y). It was issued directly from Glosters to the CU in June 1945 along with EE316 (XL-U) and EE318 (XL-Z)

Left, EE236/B belongs to the batch powered by the same engine as the F.1. It was delivered direct from Glosters at the end of December 1944 and became YQ-P. As with all of the operational F.3s, it was sent to 1335 CU in March 1945 and eventually passed on to ECFS in July where it was coded 'B' as per the photo. It was converted to an instructional airframe in January 1946. *(Andrew Thomas)*

Gloster Meteor F.3s (EE354 XL-H nearest) of No. 1335 (Meteor) Conversion Unit taxi to dispersal after a demonstration flight for the Brazilian Air Minister and his party at Molesworth, Huntingdonshire. EE354 was issued to 1335 CU in July 1945.

October 1944 by merging various units. It dealt with the development of fighter tactics and testing new fighter aircraft and equipment. It also dealt with the training of squadron and flight commanders. The CFE was divided into various squadrons, each with a specific role. Logically, the Meteor became part of its inventory with EE281, brand new and delivered from Glosters, arriving on 24 March and EE232 following on 29 March. The former's career with the CFE was short when, on 17 May, while being attached to the FIDS (Fighter Interception Development Squadron), W/C Francis S. Gonsalves, the FIDS' CO, and recently awarded the DSO for his command at the head of No. 85 Squadron, encountered an engine failure in the circuit. He lost height and crash-landed with the undercarriage and flaps down outside the airfield. Sent to Glosters, the aircraft was not repaired and became an instructional airframe. The CFE had to wait until July to see the number of Meteors increase with the arrival of EE235, EE240, EE241 and EE348 (the latter direct from Glosters) followed by EE243 in August. Other units received some Meteors, like the EFCS (Empire Central Flying School), which accepted three in July 1945 (EE231, EE236 and EE239). These were still in use when the war ended. To this, it must be added the death of Squadron Leader Alan O. Moffet on 21 July 1945. He was at that time the chief test pilot for the company Power Jets. That day he was participating to a display at the factory when he passed over the airfield of Bruntingthorpe at 500 ft at 450 knots. He then pulled up steeply into cloud. The aircraft was then seen flick rolling before levelling out inverted, it then dived into the ground near Whetstore (Leics), killing the pilot instantly. Meteor F.3 EE291 was on loan to Power Jets at that time and was never taken on RAF charge, and was the test bed for a reheated version of the RB37 engine.

The war was still underway when the RAF began to convert more squadrons to the Meteor. Number 504 (County of Nottingham) Squadron - code TM - became the second fighter squadron to transition to the Meteor F.3 when it gave up its Spitfire IXs in March 1945. Commanded by Squadron Leader M. Kellett, the first two Meteors were received on 24 March (EE280 and EE282). Within a fortnight, the full complement had arrived: EE283 to EE289, EE292 and, a bit later, EE293, EE295, EE297, EE298, EE299, EE302, EE303, EE304, EE305. Conversion training began at the end of March 1945 at Colerne. Between the 1st and 9th of April, the pilots flew Meteors with 1335 CU then their own aircraft on which 86 hours and forty minutes were logged. In May, another 190 hours were flown, which included a simulated attack on a formation of Lancasters escorted by Mustangs. The Meteor pilots 'claimed' six Lancasters and three Mustangs destroyed and admitted the loss of one Meteor to the Mustangs. Valuable lessons were learned and the Mustangs found they could get the better of the Meteors if they could be slowed down. Another 190 hours were recorded in June which also saw the loss of Flight Sergeant R.E.G. Chase on 8 June when he was killed in a flying accident. Very few hours were logged in July because the squadron made preparations to leave for Lubeck in Germany. The squadron had just started to fly again when, on 10 August, it was renamed No. 245 Squadron. This change was marked by a dramatic event that occurred on the 23rd when Squadron Leader A. Brees and Warrant Officer J. Gotlieb collided while flying in close formation over the Bristol Channel. The tail unit of Brees' aircraft was cut off, and it crashed in to the sea, but Gotlieb managed to return to base in his EE283/MR-Q. Number 74 Squadron re-equipped after the conversion of 504 Squadron. At the end of May, the squadron, which had just returned from the Continent, took charge of its first Meteor F.3s and deliveries lasted until mid-July (EE306 to EE310,

A line-up of Gloster Meteor F.3s of 74 Sqn at Colerne in the summer of 1945. Meteor 4D-Z in the foreground is EE346 and was delivered to the squadron in mid-July 1945.

EE312, EE332 to EE335, EE340 to EE346). One Meteor was lost before the end of the month, EE308, when it hit trees during a flypast rehearsal for a press demonstration. The pilot, F/Sgt J.T. Rees, lost control and was killed in the crash. When September came, one last squadron began its conversion. Number 124 Squadron had received its first Meteors the previous 27 August (EE362, EE363), followed by EE364 and EE365 and EE366. More Meteors would follow in September, but that would be officially during peacetime. When VJ-Day came, the RAF could count three operational jet fighter squadrons (74, 245 and 263) with a fourth underway (124). Deliveries would continue until December 1946 and nine more squadrons would eventually receive the F.3 as main equipment (1, 56, 66, 92, 222, 234, 257, 266 and 500). A handful of units had the F.3 on strength as interim equipment pending the arrival of the F.4.

Date	Pilot	S/N	Origin	Serial	Code	Unit	Fate
11.04.45	W/O Rodney **Marr**	Aus. 421121	RAAF	**EE234**		1335 CU	-
17.05.45	W/C Francis S. **Gonsalves**	RAF No. 86378	RAF	**EE232**		FIDS	-
18.05.45	W/C Alan S. **Dredge**	RAF No. 63785	RAF	**EE238**		1335 CU	†
08.06.45	F/Sgt Raymond E.G. **Chase**	RAF No. 1681985	RAF	**EE288**		504 Sqn	†
21.07.45	S/L Alan O. **Moffet**	RAF No. 40736	RAF	**EE291**		Power Jets	†
24.07.45	F/Sgt James T. **Rees**	RAF No. 1337576	RAF	**EE308**		74 Sqn	†
02.08.45	*ground accident*	-	-	**EE228**	XL-P	1335 CU	-
23.08.45	S/L Alec **Brees**	RAF No.106178	RAF	**EE280**		245 Sqn	†

When the war ended in September 1945, 124 Sqn was about to begin conversion to the Meteor F.3. Leading two other F.3s of the squadron, EE393/ON-J was taken on charge on 22 September.

Simplified register (Wartime period)

Serial	Available for allocation	Squadron
F.I		
EE210	Jan.44	-
EE211	Mar.44	-
EE212	Apr.44	-
EE213	May.44	-
EE214	May.44	-
EE215	Jun.44	**616**
EE216	Jun.44	**616**
EE217	Jun.44	**616**
EE218	Jul.44	**616**
EE219	Jul.44	**616** *(YQ-D, later YQ-N)*
EE220	Jul.44	**616** *(YQ-G)*
EE221	Jul.44	**616** *(YQ-C, HJW)*
EE222	Aug.44	**616** *(YQ-G)*
EE223	Nov.44	-
EE224	Aug.44	**616** *(YQ-O)*
EE225	Aug.44	**616**
EE226	Aug.44	**616**
EE227	Aug.44	**616** *(YQ-Y)*
EE228	Aug.44	**616**
EE229	Aug.44	**616** *(YQ-W)*
F.III		
EE230	Nov.44	-
EE231	Dec.44	**616**
EE232	Dec.44	**616**
EE233	Dec.44	**616**
EE234	Dec.44	**616** *(YQ-O)*
EE235	Dec.44	**616** *(YQ-C)*
EE236	Dec.44	**616** *(YQ-P)*
EE237	Dec.44	**616**
EE238	Dec.44	**616**
EE239	Mar.45	**616** *(YQ-Q)*
EE240	Jan.45	**616**
EE241	Jan.45	**616**
EE242	Jan.45	**616**
EE243	Jan.45	**616** *(YQ-F)*
EE244	Jan.45	**616**
EE245	Feb.45	**616** *(YQ-C later YQ-H)*, **263** *(HE-H)*
EE246	Feb.45	**616** *(YQ-A later YQ-J)*
EE247	Feb.45	**616** *(YQ-N)*
EE248	Feb.45	**616** *(YQ-C)*, **263** *(HE-C)*
EE249	Feb.45	**616** *(YQ-N)*, **263** *(HE-N)*
EE250	Feb.45	**616**, **263**
EE251	Feb.45	-
EE252	Feb.45	**616**
EE253	Feb.45	**616** *(YQ-F)*, **263**
EE254	Mar.45	**616**
EE269	May.45	-
EE270	Feb.45	**616**
EE271	Mar.45	**616** *(YQ-P)*, **263**
EE272	Mar.45	**616** *(YQ-M)*, **263** *(HE-M)*
EE273	Mar.45	**616**
EE274	Mar.45	**616** *(YQ-X, later YQ-P)*, **263** *(HE-X)*

EE275	Mar.45	**616** (YQ-Q), **263** (HE-Q)
EE276	Mar.45	**616** (YQ-T), **263** (HE-R)
EE277	Mar.45	**616**
EE278	Mar.45	**616**, **263** (HE-T)
EE279	Mar.45	**504**, **616**, **263** (HE-G)
EE280	Mar.45	**504**, **245**
EE281	Mar.45	-
EE282	Mar.45	**504** (TM-V), **245** (MR-B)
EE283	Mar.45	**504**, **245** (MR-Q)
EE284	Mar.45	**504**, **245** (MR-F)
EE285	Mar.45	**504**, **616** (YQ-A), **263** (HE-A)
EE286	Apr.45	**504** (TM-Q), **245** (MR-Q)
EE287	Apr.45	**504**, **245**
EE288	Apr.45	**504**
EE289	Apr.45	**504**, **245** (MR-M)
EE290	Apr.45	-
EE291	Apr.45	-
EE292	Apr.45	**504**, **245** (MR-D)
EE293	Jun.45	**504** (TM-G), **245**
EE294	Apr.45	**616**, **504**, **245** (MR-R)
EE295	Apr.45	**504**, **245** (MR-G)
EE296	Apr.45	**616**, **504**, **245** (MR-T)
EE297	May.45	**504**, **245**
EE298	May.45	**504**, **245**
EE299	May.45	**504**, **245** (MR-X)
EE300	May.45	**616** (YQ-Q), **263** (HE-K)
EE301	May.45	**616**, **263** (HE-X)
EE302	May.45	**504**, **245** (MR-J)
EE303	May.45	**504**, **245**
EE304	May.45	**504**, **245**
EE305	May.45	**504**, **245**
EE306	May.45	**74** (4D-N)
EE307	May.45	**74** (4D-B)
EE308	May.45	**74**
EE309	May.45	**74** (4D-H, later 4D-O)
EE310	Jun.45	**74** (4D-P)
EE311	Jun.45	-
EE312	Jun.45	**74**
EE313	Jun.45	-
EE314	Jun.45	-
EE315	Jun.45	-
EE316	Jun.45	-
EE317	Jun.45	**504**
EE318	Jun.45	-
EE331	Jun.45	-
EE332	Jun.45	**74**
EE333	Jun.45	**74** (4D-R)
EE334	Jun.45	**74**
EE335	Jun.45	**74**
EE336	Jul.45	-
EE337	Jun.45	-
EE338	Jun.45	-
EE339	Jul.45	-
EE340	Jun.45	**74** (4D-T)
EE341	Jul.45	**74** (4D-G)
EE342	Jul.45	**74** (4D-V later 4D-Z)
EE343	Jul.45	**74** (4D-X)
EE344	Jul.45	**74**
EE345	Jul.45	**74** (4D-K)
EE346	Jul.45	**74**

Meteor EE341/4D-G of 74 Sqn at Colerne in the summer of 1945.

EE347	Jul.45	-
EE348	Jul.45	-
EE349	Jul.45	-
EE350	Jul.45	-
EE351	Jul.45	-
EE352	Jul.45	-
EE353	Jul.45	-
EE354	Jul.45	-
EE355	Jul.45	-
EE356	Jul.45	-
EE357	Aug.45	-
EE358	Aug.45	**74** *(4D-D)*
EE359	Aug.45	-
EE360	-	Built as F.4
EE361	Aug.45	-
EE362	Aug.45	**124** *(ON-C)*
EE363	Aug.45	**124**
EE364	Aug.45	**124** *(ON-D)*
EE365	Aug.45	**124** *(ON-N)*
EE366	Aug.45	**124** *(ON-Q)*

Squadron allocation took place after VJ-Day from EE367.

IN MEMORIAM

Meteor F.1 & F.3 (wartime)

Name	Service No	Rank	Age	Origin	Date	Serial
Brees, Alec	RAF No. 106178	S/L	n/k	RAF	23.08.45	EE280
Cartmel, Brian	RAF No. 1512014	W/O	24	RAF	29.04.45	EE273
Chase, Raymond Eustace Gordon	RAF No. 1681985	F/Sgt	22	RAF	08.06.45	EE288
Davie, William Douglas Bow Symington	RAF No. 72481	S/L	25	RAF	04.01.44	DG204
Dredge, Allan Sydney	RAF No. 63785	W/C	27	RAF	18.05.45	EE238
Gregg, Donald Arthur	RAF No. 1235043	W/O	21	RAF	15.08.44	EE226
Moffet, Alan Ormerod	RAF No. 40736	S/L	25	RAF	21.07.45	EE291
Rees, James Thomas	RAF No. 1337576	F/Sgt	23	RAF	24.07.45	EE308
Watts, Leslie William	RAF No. 117728	S/L	28	RAF	29.04.45	EE252

Total: 9

United Kingdom: 9

Meteor EE214/G was one of the Mk. Is used as a test bed but before that it briefly served, on loan, with 616 Sqn to help convert the pilots to the type and, for about five weeks, was coded YQ-B. It is here seen during a later test flight with a ventral fuel tank.

Gloster Meteor F. I EE221/G
No. 616 (South Yorkshire) Squadron
Wing Commander Hugh 'Willie' WILSON
Manston (UK), Summer 1944

Gloster Meteor F. I EE214/G
No. 616 (South Yorkshire) Squadron
Manston (UK), Summer 1944

Gloster Meteor F. I EE222/G
No. 616 (South Yorkshire) Squadron
Wing Commander Andrew 'Andy' McDOWALL
Manston (UK), Summer 1944

Gloster Meteor F. 3 EE247
No. 616 (South Yorkshire) Squadron
B.158/Lübeck (Germany), Summer 1945

N.B.: This Meteor was christened 'Angela' (below the windscreen)

Gloster Meteor F. 3 EE341
No. 74 (Trinidad) Squadron
Colerne (UK), Summer 1945

SQUADRONS! - The series

1. The Supermarine Spitfire Mk VI
2. The Republic Thunderbolt Mk I
3. The Supermarine Spitfire Mk V in the Far East
4. The Boeing Fortress Mk I
5. The Supermarine Spitfire Mk XII
6. The Supermarine Spitfire Mk VII
7. The Supermarine Spitfire F. 21
8. The Handley Page Halifax Mk I
9. The Forgotten Fighters
10. The NA Mustang IV in Western Europe
11. The NA Mustang IV over the Balkans and Italy
12. The Supermarine Spitfire Mk XVI - *The British*
13. The Martin Marauder Mk I
14. The Supermarine Spitfire Mk VIII in the Southwest Pacific - *The British*
15. The Gloster Meteor F.I & F.III
16. The NA Mitchell - *The Dutch, Poles and French*
17. The Curtiss Mohawk
18. The Curtiss Kittyhawk Mk II
19. The Boulton Paul Defiant - *day and night fighter*
20. The Supermarine Spitfire Mk VIII in the Southwest Pacific - *The Australians*
21. The Boeing Fortress Mk II & Mk III
22. The Douglas Boston and Havoc - *The Australians*
23. The Republic Thunderbolt Mk II
24. The Douglas Boston and Havoc - *Night fighters*
25. The Supermarine Spitfire Mk V - *The Eagles*
26. The Hawker Hurricane - *The Canadians*
27. The Supermarine Spitfire Mk V - *The 'Bombay' squadrons*
28. The Consolidated Liberator - *The Australians*
29. The Supermarine Spitfire Mk XVI - *The Dominions*
30. The Supermarine Spitfire Mk V - *The Belgian and Dutch squadrons*
31. The Supermarine Spitfire Mk V - *The New-Zealanders*
32. The Supermarine Spitfire Mk V - *The Norwegians*
33. The Brewster Buffalo
34. The Supermarine Spitfire Mk II - *The Foreign squadrons*
35. The Martin Marauder Mk II
36. The Supermarine Spitfire Mk V - *The Special Reserve squadrons*
37. The Supermarine Spitfire Mk XIV - *The Belgian and Dutch squadrons*
38. The Supermarine Spitfire Mk II - *The Rhodesian, Dominion & Eagle squadrons*
39. The Douglas Boston and Havoc - *Intruders*
40. The North American Mustang Mk III over Italy and the Balkans (Pt-1)
41. The Bristol Brigand
42. The Supermarine Spitfire Mk V - *The Australians*
43. The Hawker Typhoon - *The Rhodesian squadrons*
44. The Supermarine Spitfire F.22 & F.24
45. The Supermarine Spitfire Mk IX - *The Belgian and Dutch squadrons*
46. The North American & CAC Mustang - *The RAAF*
47. The Westland Whirlwind
48. The Supermarine Spitfire Mk XIV - *The British squadrons*
49. The Supermarine Spitfire Mk I - *The beginning (the Auxiliary squadrons)*
50. The Hawker Tempest Mk V - *The New Zealanders*
51. The Last of the Long-Range Biplane Flying Boats
52. The Supermarine Spitfire Mk IX - *The Former Canadian Homefront squadrons*
53. The Hawker Hurricane Mk I & Mk II - *The Eagle squadrons*
54. The Hawker biplane fighters
55. The Supermarine Spitfire Mk IX - *The Auxiliary squadrons*
56. The Hawker Typhoon - *The Canadian squadrons*
57. The Douglas SBD - *New Zealand and France*
58. The Forgotten Patrol Seaplanes
59. The Dutch Fighter Squadrons - *Nos. 322 & 120 (NEI) Squadrons*
60. The Supermarine Spitfire - *The Australian Squadrons in Western Europe and the Med*
61. The Belgian Fighter Squadrons - *Nos. 349 & 350 Squadrons*
62. The Supermarine Spitfire Mk I - *The beginning (the Regular squadrons)*
63. The Hawker Typhoon - *The 'Fellowship of the Bellows' squadrons*
64. The North American Mustang Mk I & Mk II
65. The Eagle Squadrons *Nos. 71, 121 & 133 Squadrons*
66. The Handley Page Hampden *Torpedo-bomber*
67. The North American Mustang Mk III over Italy and the Balkans (Pt-2)

www.ingramcontent.com/pod-product-compliance
Lightning Source LLC
Chambersburg PA
CBHW060824090426
42738CB00002B/94